DC
COMICS™

W9-BPO-738

BATPLANES
AND
BATCOPTERS
THE ENGINEERING BEHIND
BATMAN'S WINGS

BY TAMMY ENZ

BATMAN CREATED BY
BOB KANE

BATMAN
SCIENCE™

CAPSTONE PRESS
a capstone imprint

Published by Capstone Press in 2014
A Capstone Imprint
1710 Roe Crest Drive
North Mankato, Minnesota 56003
www.capstonepub.com

Copyright © 2014 DC Comics
BATMAN and all related characters and elements are trademarks of and © DC Comics.
(s14)

STAR30445

No part of this publication may be reproduced in whole or in part, or stored in a retrieval system,
or transmitted in any form or by any means, electronic, mechanical, photocopying, recording, or
otherwise, without written permission.

Library of Congress Cataloging-in-Publication Data
Cataloging-in-publication information is on file with the Library of Congress.
ISBN 978-1-4765-3941-6 (library binding)
ISBN 978-1-4765-5209-5 (paperback)

Summary: Explores the real-world science and engineering connections to the features in
Batman's aircraft.

Editorial Credits
Editor: Christopher L. Harbo
Designer: Veronica Scott
Production Specialist: Kathy McColley

Photo Credits
Central Intelligence Agency, 23; Getty Images: Time Life Pictures/Joseph Scherschel, 22; LaserMotive,
Inc., 17 (bottom); Library of Congress, 6; NASA Dryden Flight Research Center: Steve Lighthill,
9 (bottom); Newscom: akg-images, 28, Reuters/Morris Mac Matzen, 7 (bottom); Shutterstock:
Christopher Parypa, 9 (top), MO_SES, 7 (top), Olga Gabay, 29 PerseoMedusa, 19 (bottom); U.S.
Air Force photo, 14; U.S. Army photo by George Kenneth Lucey Jr. and Benson King, 19 (top); U.S.
Marine Corps photo by Cpl. Garry J. Welch, 15, Cpl. Justin M. Boling, 17 (top); U.S. Navy photo, 13
(bottom), MC2 Brian Morales, 13 (top), MC2 Julio Rivera, 27, MC3 Mark El-Rayes, 10, MCSN Timothy
A. Hazel, 21, PH3 Joshua Karsten, 20; Wikimedia: Carla Cioffi, 25 (top); Wikipedia: Bernd.Brincken,
11, Gryffinder, 8, J Clear, 25 (top)

Design Elements: Shutterstock: BiterBig, ClickHere, Jason Winter

Printed in the United States of America in Stevens Point, Wisconsin.
102013   007767WZS14

TABLE OF CONTENTS

SUPER HERO WINGS

The Caped Crusader commands the skies. While his cape helps him glide, Batman's flying machines send him soaring. Batplanes and Batcopters are absolutely essential crime-fighting tools for the Dark Knight.

For decades Batman has designed his amazing planes, helicopters, and other aircraft to fit his adventurous needs. But no matter when he flies, all of these air vehicles have been packed with cool gadgets and technology. From vertical takeoffs to guided missiles, Batman's planes and helicopters rule Gotham City's skies.

But is Batman's awesome flying technology limited to super heroes? Could scientists and engineers ever hope to design machines as cool as his?

The Batplane and Batcopter have many advanced features, but they're not all science fiction. Batman's aircraft use an amazing amount of real technology. And much of it has been around for years. Need proof? Get ready to explore the real-world science and engineering behind Batman's planes and helicopters.

CHAPTER 1

PERFORMANCE

Batplanes and Batcopters seem to fly like no other aircraft. With sleek shapes, jet-powered engines, and spinning blades they handle the harshest conditions.

AERODYNAMICS

There's no mistaking the Batplane. Its black body and wings make it look like a bat in flight. But is its design for looks or for function? The answer is a little of both.

Most real aircraft look similar to animals in flight. In particular, airplanes look like soaring birds or flying bats—and for good reason. Early studies in **aerodynamics** were based on bird flight. In the 1890s German engineer Otto Lilienthal built gliders by studying bird wings. Aircraft today still use his designs for wing shapes.

Otto Lilienthal tests one of his gliders in 1895.

aerodynamics—the ability of something to move easily and quickly through the air

Modern airplane wings are rounded on the front and tapered toward the back. As an airplane moves, this shape allows air to flow faster over the top of the wings. At the same time, air moves slower under the wings. The unequal pressure pushes the plane upward. This pressure is called lift. A pilot changes the amount of lift by adjusting flaps on the wings. These flaps also allow the airplane to turn and slow down for landings.

SMART BIRD

Airplane wings can't flap like a bird's wings. But engineers at the German company Festo are changing that. They have designed the Smart Bird. This robotic bird has a 6.5-foot (2-meter) wingspan. It flaps its wings like a seagull. The Smart Bird may one day lead to new engineering designs for manned aircraft.

SUPERSONIC JETS

When enemy missiles lock onto the Batplane, the Dark Knight needs all the speed he can get. Luckily, jet engines power his aircraft. Not only does he outrun enemy fire, but he also shatters the speed of sound.

Jet powered aircraft got their start in 1939. The first jet plane was a German designed Heinkel He 178. Its top speed was 373 miles (600 kilometers) per hour. Since then, all jet engines use the same basic idea. Their power comes from injecting and burning fuel in an engine chamber. As the fuel burns, rapidly expanding gases burst from the engine. These gases create the **thrust** that pushes the plane forward.

Heinkel He 178

Some modern jets travel so fast they break the speed of sound. But traveling faster than 768 miles (1,236 km) per hour has a drawback. It creates an earsplitting sonic boom. A sonic boom happens when a jet suddenly shoves air **molecules** out of its way. The shock waves that result sound like loud thunder. The larger the plane and the closer it flies to the ground, the louder the boom. A boom can be so loud that it can hurt people's eardrums or damage buildings.

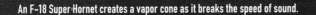

An F-18 Super Hornet creates a vapor cone as it breaks the speed of sound.

LYNX SPACECRAFT

XCOR Aerospace has a new plan for supersonic flight. Its *Lynx* spacecraft will take off from a runway much like a normal plane. Rocket engines will lift the spacecraft almost straight up. They will take the *Lynx* outside Earth's atmosphere for short space flights. Then the spacecraft will glide back down to the runway. For $100,000 space tourists can already start booking future *Lynx* flights.

FACT:

NASA'S X-43A SET THE WORLD RECORD AS THE FASTEST AIRCRAFT ON NOVEMBER 16, 2004. IT REACHED A SPEED OF NEARLY 7,000 MILES (11,265 KM) PER HOUR.

thrust—the force that pushes a vehicle forward

molecule—the atoms making up the smallest unit of a substance

ROTOR POWER

Speed and power can only get Batman so far in the Batplane. To move around in tight areas, he needs the **rotor** power of the Batcopter. Rotors allow this whirlybird to sneak between skyscrapers or land on a busy street.

In the real world, helicopters use rotors to lift off and land in places airplanes can't. The science behind a helicopter's rotors is the key to its flight. A helicopter has two sets of rotors. The main rotor on top has large blades that slice through the air. They create lift that allows the helicopter to rise. The smaller rotor on the helicopter's tail balances out the main rotor. Without the tail rotor, a helicopter would spin out of control.

Spinning rotors allow an MH-60S Seahawk helicopter to hover above a ship's deck.

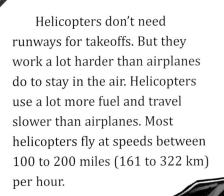

Helicopters don't need runways for takeoffs. But they work a lot harder than airplanes do to stay in the air. Helicopters use a lot more fuel and travel slower than airplanes. Most helicopters fly at speeds between 100 to 200 miles (161 to 322 km) per hour.

EUROCOPTER X3

The Eurocopter X3 uses a unique rotor design. This experimental helicopter has rotors on its sides. These rotors help keep the helicopter stable. They also allow it to gain more speed than a regular helicopter. The X3 reaches top speeds of about 270 miles (435 km) per hour.

rotor—the system of rotating blades on a helicopter; a rotor provides force to lift a helicopter into the air

Flying above Gotham City's streets is more dangerous than driving on them. Batman must weave between skyscrapers and hover in midair. Fortunately, the Batplane and Batcopter are up to the task.

SHORT TAKEOFFS AND LANDINGS

The Batplane has touched down on a busy city street. But with no runway, there's no way the aircraft can take off. Or is there? The Batplane suddenly lifts itself into the sky. Who needs long runways with the ability to take off from tight spaces?

In the real world, most airplanes need about 2,300 feet (700 m) of runway to take off and land. But fighter jets on aircraft carriers only use about 300 feet (90 m). How can they use such short runways?

For most fighter jets, **catapults** and tail hooks are the key. For takeoffs, the jet's front wheels hook to a catapult cable. The pilot revs the plane's engines to full throttle. Then a high-pressure **piston** pulls the plane down the runway. It flings the jet off the aircraft carrier. The plane reaches 170 miles (274 km) per hour in just two seconds!

An F-18 Super Hornet traps an arresting cable as it lands on the deck of an aircraft carrier.

Landing on an aircraft carrier is one of the riskiest tasks for a fighter jet pilot. The pilot must use the jet's tail hook to trap an arresting cable stretched across the ship's deck. In the landing approach, the pilot pushes the jet to full power. If the tail hook misses the cable, the pilot heads back into the air. If the tail hook traps the cable, the jet slows down rapidly.

FACT:

LAUNCHING AIRCRAFT OFF SHIPS DATES BACK TO WORLD WAR I (1914-1918). THE NAVY CATAPULTED ITS FIRST AIRCRAFT OFF THE USS *NORTH CAROLINA* ON NOVEMBER 5, 1915.

catapult—a hydraulic device used to launch airplanes from the deck of a ship

piston—a part inside a hydraulic machine that moves up and down, expanding and compressing fluid

13

GOING VERTICAL

Short takeoffs and landings are amazing. But what if you have no runway at all? The Batplane's **vertical** takeoffs and landings seem impossible for a plane. But the Ryan X-13 Vertijet and the Harrier Jump Jet prove otherwise.

The tail-sitting Ryan X-13 Vertijet mastered vertical takeoffs and landings more the 50 years ago. This small jet was called a tail-sitter. It took off and landed on its tail. The plane was designed to launch from a submarine. The Vertijet made history on April 11, 1957. A pilot launched it like a rocket, but flew it like a plane. Then he landed the Vertijet back on its tail. Because the Vertijet was difficult to land, only two **prototypes** were built and tested. But the plane paved the way for the Harrier Jump Jet.

The Harrier Jump Jet first took to the skies in the late 1960s. Its thrusters direct power from the jet engines downward. This downward thrust allows the Harrier to make completely vertical takeoffs and landings. Once airborne, the pilot changes the thrusters' angle and power for normal flight.

A Ryan X-13 Vertijet comes in for a landing.

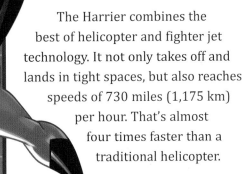

The Harrier combines the best of helicopter and fighter jet technology. It not only takes off and lands in tight spaces, but also reaches speeds of 730 miles (1,175 km) per hour. That's almost four times faster than a traditional helicopter.

A night-vision camera captures the vertical thrust of the Harrier Jump Jet as it lands.

vertical—straight up and down

prototype—the first version of an invention that tests an idea to see if it will work

HOVERING

Batman hovers over Gotham City in the Batcopter. With such convenient midair parking, keeping an eye out for criminal activity is a cinch. But how do real helicopters manage to stay in place high in the air?

We've all seen helicopters hover above the ground. This ability is important in rescue missions and when loading and unloading cargo.

Hovering in midair isn't easy. **Gravity** always pulls the helicopter toward the ground. In addition, wind gusts push the helicopter around. To stay in one spot, pilots constantly adjust the rotor controls to balance these forces.

With all of these forces acting on a helicopter, is it possible to hover without a pilot? On May 22, 2012, U.S. marines completed the first "hot hook up" using a K-MAX unmanned helicopter. As the unpiloted helicopter hovered overhead, marines attached cargo to a cable hanging from the craft. Unlike other unmanned air vehicles, K-MAXs aren't flown remotely by a pilot on the ground. They fly almost completely by themselves based on programmed instructions.

A K-MAX unmanned helicopter prepares for takeoff in Afghanistan.

LASER HOVERING

LaserMotive, a Seattle-based company, has developed a small model helicopter that hovers with the help of a laser beam. From the ground, the laser is aimed at power cells under the helicopter. The power cells change the laser light into electricity. With this power, the rotors keep the mini aircraft hovering in the air.

gravity—a force that pulls objects with mass together; gravity pulls objects down toward the center of Earth

CHAPTER 3

ENEMY ENGAGEMENT

In Batman's quest for justice, he disables enemies with a variety of weapons. The Batcopter's whirling vortex stomps out riots. The Batplane's guided missiles disable targets with precision.

VORTEX WEAPONS

Gotham City's police force is no match for a raging mob. But Batman has things under control. He uses the Batcopter's **vortex** to control the situation. This swirling downdraft from the rotors forces rioters to the ground.

The military and police forces work on developing nonlethal weapons that disable targets. In fact, the U.S. military developed and studied a vortex ring gun for crowd control in 1998. This weapon sent out a high-speed ring of air.

Researchers test the strength of a vortex ring gun for the military.

The ring was powerful enough to knock down a 150-pound (68-kg) mannequin 30 feet (9 m) away. The military also studied adding pepper spray to the shock wave to strengthen its punch. While the vortex ring gun worked, it wasn't precise enough for real-world use.

The military may have shelved its device, but vortex technology is used to solve other real life problems. A hail cannon blasts storm clouds with shock waves to prevent hailstones from forming. Why prevent hailstones? Millions of dollars worth of crops are destroyed each year by hail. Explosive gases inside a hail cannon fire 200-mile (322-km) per hour shock waves into thunderstorms. These waves seek to break up hail before it hits tender crops and fragile greenhouses. But do hail cannons really work? Scientists have their doubts, but many farmers believe they do.

A hail canon stands ready to protect a vineyard from hail.

vortex—air moving in a circular motion

PRECISION MISSILES

As a defender of justice, Batman protects the lives of innocent people and criminals alike. His goal is always to disarm his enemies. To do that, the missiles on his aircraft are very precise. They only seek out and lock onto the targets Batman wants to strike.

Precision guided missiles are called smart bombs. They are programmed or steered toward their target. Modern smart bombs include Television/**Infrared** (TV/IR) bombs, laser-guided missiles, Joint Direct Attack Munitions (JDAM), and heat-seeking missiles.

A TV/IR bomb has a TV or an infrared camera mounted to its nose. The camera sends video to a controller. The controller uses the video to steer the bomb toward its target.

A sailor performs final maintenance on a JDAM bomb prior to a flight mission.

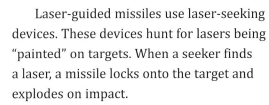

Laser-guided missiles use laser-seeking devices. These devices hunt for lasers being "painted" on targets. When a seeker finds a laser, a missile locks onto the target and explodes on impact.

JDAMs are guidance kits. They change regular bombs into smart bombs. JDAM bombs are each programmed with the **GPS** coordinates for their targets. Up to 80 JDAMs can drop from a plane in one pass. Each one can seek out a different target.

Heat-seeking missiles are used for air-to-air combat. A heat-seeker senses the heat from an enemy aircraft. It guides itself toward this heat source before exploding.

FACT:

THE SIDEWINDER HEAT-SEEKING MISSILE IS 9 FEET, 5 INCHES (3.4 M) LONG. IT WEIGHS 188 POUNDS (85 KG). IT CAN TRAVEL MORE THAN 10 MILES (16 KM) TO ITS TARGET. EACH SIDEWINDER COSTS ABOUT $84,000.

infrared—light waves in the electromagnetic spectrum between visible light and microwaves

GPS—an electronic tool used to find the location of an object; GPS stands for Global Positioning System

The Batplane and Batcopter have a mix of tricks to help the Dark Knight do his job. From airlifts to ejection systems, Batman's aircraft have solutions for nearly every situation.

SKYHOOK

When Batman gets backed into a corner, the only way out is up. In these situations his air vehicles come to the rescue. In mid-flight, they use ladders and cables to pluck the Caped Crusader right off the ground.

Rescue workers use helicopters to airlift injured climbers off mountains every year. But what about being lifted off the ground by a plane flying at 125 miles (200 km) per hour? It sounds like science fiction, but it's not. In the 1960s the Central Intelligence Agency (CIA) began using Skyhook. This system allowed a low-flying plane to pluck people off the ground without ever landing.

A Navy sailor is lifted out of the water during testing of the Skyhook system.

To perform a Skyhook rescue, a packet was airdropped to a person on the ground. Inside were a harness, a high-strength nylon rope, and a weather balloon. The person on the ground hooked himself into the harness. The balloon was inflated using a portable helium bottle. The balloon pulled the 500-foot (152-m) rope into the air. Then a passing plane snagged the rope with forks attached to its nose. After releasing the weather balloon, the passenger was reeled onboard the back of the plane with a winch.

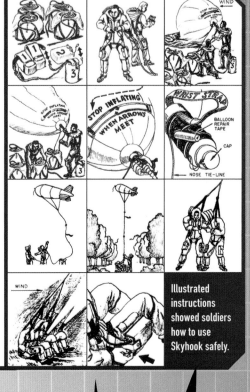

Illustrated instructions showed soldiers how to use Skyhook safely.

OPERATION COLDFEET

In 1962 Operation Coldfeet became the first official mission to use Skyhook. The CIA successfully pulled two people from the arctic ice. They had been exploring an abandoned Soviet Union ice station.

EJECTION SYSTEM

The Batplane just took a hit. It's spiraling out of the sky. Is this the end of the line for the Dark Knight? No way. Batman's ejection system propels him to safety.

Many military aircraft have ejection systems. When activated, an aircraft's system blasts the top off the cockpit. A rocket motor launches the seat into the air to get the pilot safely away from the plane. Sensors track his or her altitude, opening parachutes and releasing the seat at a safe height. If landing over water, a survival kit drops down with a self-inflating life jacket and raft attached.

Some aircraft fly so high they need escape pods to help pilots survive in the thin, cold air. One of the first aircraft escape pods was installed in the B-58 Hustler in the 1960s. The pods could eject a flight crew traveling twice the speed of sound at 70,000 feet (21,000 m) above Earth. They sealed each crew member into clamlike capsules with their own oxygen. Parachutes released to help the pods land safely. If they landed in water, the clamshells opened to become floating rafts.

The B-58 Hustler's escape pods sealed crew members up in clamlike capsules.

SPACE ESCAPE POD

Escape pods are very important for space travel. Astronauts wouldn't survive a disaster without a navigable escape pod. The *International Space Station* always has a Russian-built *Soyuz* escape pod ready for speedy escapes. This three-person pod can support life for up to three days.

The top of a *Soyuz* rocket holds the escape pod used on the *International Space Station*.

Batman's aircraft take the Caped Crusader where few others can go. To do that, they sometimes use the best of both airplane and helicopter technology.

HELICOPTER AND AIRPLANE

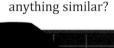

Is it a helicopter? Is it an airplane? Sometimes Batman's aircraft act like both. They take off and land like helicopters. But they also fly fast like jets. Does the real world have anything similar?

The U.S. military began developing aircraft that could work like a helicopter and an airplane in the 1950s. These efforts paid off when the Bell Boeing V-22 Osprey took flight in 1989. It was the world's first tilt-rotor.

The Osprey is called a tilt-rotor because its rotors tilt. Tilting rotors allow it to change from helicopter-mode to airplane-mode in mid-flight. When the Osprey's rotors swing vertically, the aircraft flies like a helicopter. When the rotors turn horizontally, they become airplane propellers. The Osprey changes from helicopter to airplane in as little as 12 seconds.

The Osprey travels twice as fast as a typical helicopter. It can carry up to 20,000 pounds (9,072 kg) of cargo or 24 soldiers. It is easily stored on aircraft carriers. Its rotors fold up and its wings rotate. The military uses the Osprey on assault and rescue missions.

Osprey prepare to take off vertically from the deck of a ship.

AUTOGYRO

Every so often Batman flies an aircraft so strange you'd think it must be pure fiction. For instance, in early adventures Batman buzzed around in a one-man Bat-Gyro. But what was this strange vehicle and is it real?

Autogyros, also called gyroplanes, are neither science fiction nor old-fashioned. These lightweight vehicles look like helicopters. They can even perform many of the same tasks as helicopters. But they fly more like airplanes.

Spanish engineer Juan de la Cierva invented the autogyro in 1920. Later helicopter designs used Cierva's ideas. An autogyro's engine and its smaller propeller push it through the air. Unlike a helicopter, an engine doesn't power its main rotor. This rotor is angled to catch air currents and provide lift.

Juan de la Cierva stands with one of his early autogyros.

Autogyros are efficient and low cost. Police officers and soldiers use them for rescue missions. They also can carry mobile medical labs. Autogyros can even be fitted with skis to land on snow or floats to land on water.

A modern two-person autogyro soars high above the ground.

EVOLVING AIRCRAFT

For the Caped Crusader, the Batplane and Batcopter represent power over the skies of Gotham City. They also serve as a reminder of the real science and engineering in today's world. What new gadgets will the Dark Knight use in his planes and helicopters next? No one knows for sure. But keep an eye on real-world science and engineering. They'll likely show up on Batman's aircraft.

GLOSSARY

aerodynamics (air-oh-dye-NA-miks)—the ability of something to move easily and quickly through the air

catapult (KAT-uh-puhlt)—a hydraulic device used to launch airplanes from the deck of a ship

GPS—an electronic tool used to find the location of an object; GPS stands for Global Positioning System

gravity (GRAV-uh-tee)—a force that pulls objects with mass together; gravity pulls objects down toward the center of Earth

infrared (in-fruh-RED)—light waves in the electromagnetic spectrum between visible light and microwaves

molecule (MOL-uh-kyool)—the atoms making up the smallest unit of a substance; H_2O is a molecule of water

piston (PIS-tuhn)—a part inside a hydraulic machine that moves up and down, expanding and compressing fluid

prototype (PROH-tuh-tipe)—the first version of an invention that tests an idea to see if it will work

rotor (ROH-tur)—the system of rotating blades on a helicopter; a rotor provides force to lift a helicopter into the air

thrust (THRUHST)—the force that pushes a vehicle forward

vertical (VUR-tuh-kuhl)—straight up and down

vortex (VOHR-tex)—air moving in a circular motion

READ MORE

Aloian, Molly. *Hovering Helicopters.* Vehicles on the Move. New York: Crabtree Pub. Co., 2011.

Boothroyd, Jennifer. *How Do Helicopters Work?* Lightning Bolt Books. Minneapolis: Lerner Publications Co., 2013.

Gregory, Josh. *From Birds to ... Aircraft.* Innovations from Nature. Ann Arbor, Mich.: Cherry Lake Publishing, 2013.

Harrison, Paul. *Superplanes.* Mean Machines. Mankato, Minn.: Arcturus Pub., 2012.

Solway, Andrew. *Aircraft.* Science and Technology. Chicago: Raintree, 2012.

INTERNET SITES

FactHound offers a safe, fun way to find Internet sites related to this book. All of the sites on FactHound have been researched by our staff.

Here's all you do:

Visit **www.facthound.com**

Type in this code: 9781476539416

www.FACTHOUND.com

INDEX